Graaes K-4

FOCUS ON ELEMENTARY GEOLOGY

Laboratory Workbook

Rebecca W. Keller, PhD

Illustrations: Janet Moneymaker
Marjie Bassler

Copyright © 2014 Gravitas Publications, Inc.

All rights reserved. No part of this publication may be reproduced, stored in a retrieval system, or transmitted, in any form or by any means, electronic, mechanical, photocopying, recording, or otherwise, without prior written permission from the publisher.

Focus On Elementary Geology Laboratory Workbook
ISBN: 978-1-936114-90-0

Published by Gravitas Publications, Inc.
www.gravitaspublications.com

Printed in United States

A Note From the Author

Hi!

In this curriculum you are going to learn the first step of the scientific method:

Making good observations!

In geology making good observations is very important.

Each experiment in this workbook is divided into several different sections. In the *Think About It* section you will answer questions, and in the *Observe It* section you will make observations about your experiment. In the *What Did You Discover?* section, you will write down or draw what you observed in the experiment. There is a section called *Why?* where you will learn about why you may have observed certain things. And finally, there is a section called *Just For Fun* that has an extra activity for you to experiment with.

These experiments will help you learn the first step of the scientific method, and ... they're lots of fun!

Enjoy!

Rebecca W. Keller, PhD

Contents

Experiment 1

Geology Every Day

Even before geology became a science, people observed rocks and landscapes, mountains, lakes, and rivers. In this experiment you will make observations about how geology affects your daily life.

I. Think About It

Think about where you live.

❶ Do you live in a city or in the country?

_____

❷ Is your house built with concrete, stone, or brick?

_____

❸ Where did the builders find the concrete, stone, or brick for your house?

_____

_____

_____

❹ Do you live near mountains or on the plains? Near a lake, an ocean, or in a desert?

_____

_____

_____

❺ What is the weather like where you live? Do you have lots of rain, tornadoes, or hurricanes?

_____

_____

_____

❻ Do you live near a volcano? Are there earthquakes where you live?

_____

_____

_____

❼ How much does the geology of where you live affect your life?

_____

_____

_____

_____

_____

_____

II. Observe It

❶ Make a list of all the geological features you see in a day, such as mountains, rivers, lakes, or an ocean.

_____

_____

_____

_____

_____

_____

❷ Observe the weather where you live and write down what you experience—hot weather, cold weather, rain, fog, snow, drought, etc.

_____

_____

_____

_____

_____

_____

❸ List the kinds of animals that live near you. Write down the names of any wildlife that you see, such as foxes, coyotes, squirrels, snakes, lizards, ants, bears, or any other kind of wildlife.

_____

_____

_____

_____

_____

_____

❹ List the types of plants that live near you. Write down the plants that grow around your home, such as green grass, flowers, cactus, or weeds.

_____

_____

_____

_____

_____

III. What Did You Discover?

❶ Do the mountains, rivers, oceans, or plains affect the kinds of wildlife you see? Why or why not?

_____

_____

_____

❷ Does the weather affect the mountains, rivers, or oceans? Why or why not?

_____

_____

_____

❸ Does the kind of soil you live near affect what kinds of plants can grow? Why or why not?

_____

_____

_____

❹ Does the area where you live affect the kind of house you live in? Why or why not?

_____

_____

_____

IV. Why?

If you live near a volcano, or if the place where you live experiences earthquakes, you might be very aware of the geology around you. However, it is easy to forget that geology affects our daily lives even without earthquakes and volcanoes. Where your house is located, the kind of plants and animals you see, the weather you experience, and the view from your house are all determined by geology.

V. Just For Fun

Imagine what it might be like to live on the Moon. What would the landscape look like—flat, mountainous, or...? Where would you want your house to be located? What would it be made of? Would you have any weather? Would you see animals and plants, and if so, what kinds?

On the next page, draw a picture of your home on the Moon.

Home on the Moon

Experiment 2

Smashing Hammers

I. Think About It

❶ What do you think will happen if you smash a banana with a plastic hammer?

_____

_____

❷ What do you think will happen if you smash a hardboiled egg with a metal hammer?

_____

_____

❸ Which do you think would work better for smashing a potato, a plastic hammer or a metal hammer? Why?

_____

_____

❹ What is inside a hardboiled egg? Is it hard or soft?

_____

_____

❺ What is inside a rock? Is it hard or soft?

_____

_____

❻ Is a banana soft or hard?

_____

_____

II. Observe It

❶ Take the plastic hammer and smash a piece of banana. In the box below, write or draw what happens.

❷ Take the metal hammer and smash another piece of banana. In the box below, write or draw what happens.

❸ Take the plastic hammer and smash a hardboiled egg. In the box below, write or draw what happens.

❹ Take the metal hammer and smash another hardboiled egg. In the box below, write or draw what happens.

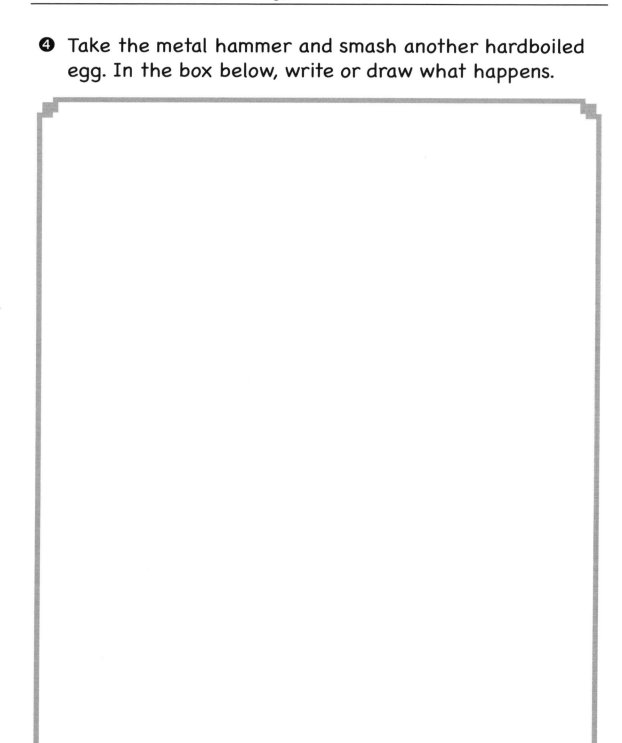

❺ Take the plastic hammer and smash a potato.
  In the box below, write or draw what happens.

❻ Take the metal hammer and smash another potato. In the box below, write or draw what happens.

❼ Take the plastic hammer and smash a rock. In the box below, write or draw what happens.

❽ Take the metal hammer and smash another rock.
In the box below, write or draw what happens.

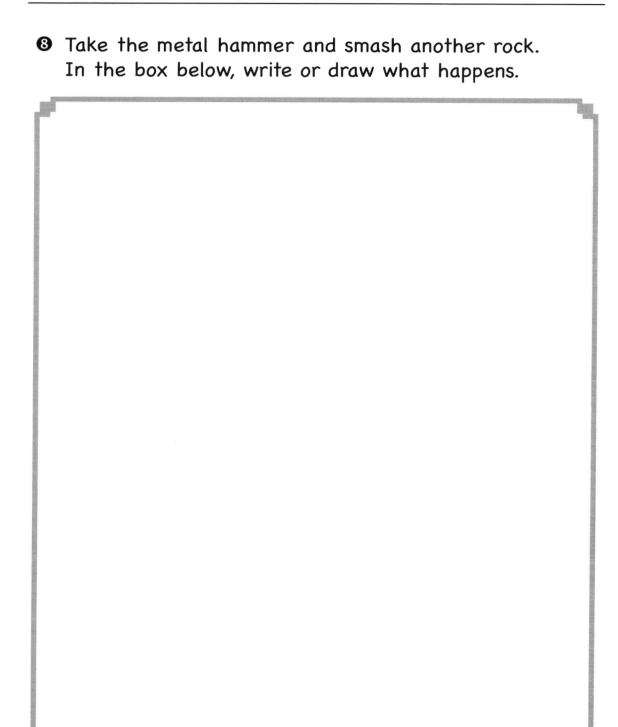

III. What Did You Discover?

❶ What happened when you used the plastic hammer to smash a banana?

_____

_____

_____

❷ What happened when you used the metal hammer to smash a banana?

_____

_____

_____

❸ What did you discover when you used the plastic hammer to smash a hardboiled egg?

_____

_____

_____

❹ What did you discover when you used the metal hammer to smash a hardboiled egg?

_____

_____

_____

❺ What did you discover when you used the plastic hammer to smash a potato?

_____

_____

_____

❻ What did you discover when you used the metal hammer to smash a potato?

_____

_____

_____

❼ What did you discover when you used the plastic hammer to smash a rock?

_____

_____

_____

❽ What did you discover when you used the metal hammer to smash a rock?

_____

_____

_____

IV. Why?

Geologists use different tools to study rocks, minerals, and Earth's layers. When a geologist needs to break open a rock to see what's inside, a rock hammer is the most commonly used tool. Smaller rock hammers that are lightweight can help geologists break open small rocks while preserving delicate gems or other structures. Larger rock hammers could destroy these small features.

Larger, heavier rock hammers are good for breaking open bigger rocks to expose fossils or larger gem structures. Smaller rock hammers might not be heavy enough to break open these bigger rocks.

In this experiment you used two different types of hammers—a lightweight plastic hammer and a heavier metal hammer. You probably discovered that the lightweight plastic hammer was able to smash the softer items and the heavier metal hammer could smash both the softer and the harder items.

A geologist will choose a lightweight hammer to break open smaller or softer rocks and a heavyweight hammer to break open bigger and harder rocks. Practice makes it easier for a geologist to choose the right hammer to use with a particular rock sample.

V. Just For Fun

Use a magnifying glass or hand lens to examine the objects you smashed in this experiment. Write or draw what you observe.

BANANA
Unsmashed
Smashed With Plastic Hammer
Smashed With Metal Hammer

HARDBOILED EGG

Unsmashed

Smashed With Plastic Hammer

Smashed With Metal Hammer

POTATO

Unsmashed

Smashed With Plastic Hammer

Smashed With Metal Hammer

ROCK

Unsmashed

Smashed With Plastic Hammer

Smashed With Metal Hammer

Experiment 3

Mud Pies

I. Observe It

❶ Go outside to your backyard, a park, or some other place where there is dirt that can be collected. Using a small shovel, dig a sample of the dirt and put it into a small pail or plastic container.

❷ Look through the dirt sample you collected. In the space below, draw what you observe.

❸ Using your hands, separate the dirt from any small or large rocks you collected in your sample.

❹ Notice that rocks are different from dirt. Explain, write, or draw how you can tell the difference between rocks and dirt.

_____

_____

_____

❺ Take about .25 liter (1 cup) of the dirt mixture and put it in a tall, clear glass or plastic container. Pour water into the container so that it covers the dirt completely. Make sure that there is 5-8 centimeters (2-3 inches) of water above the dirt.

❻ Stir the dirt gently with your fingers. Watch what happens to the water that was above the dirt and observe what happens to the rocks. Write or draw your observations below.

_____

_____

_____

❼ Allow the mixture to settle. Observe what happens and write or draw your observations below.

_____

_____

_____

II. Think About It

❶ Can you tell the difference between rocks and dirt? If so, can you explain the difference?

_____

_____

_____

_____

_____

❷ When you added water to the dirt, mixed it up, and allowed it settle, what did you observe?

_____

_____

_____

_____

_____

❸ Add 60 milliliters (1/4 cup) of flour to the mixture. Stir the mixture and allow it to settle. Observe what happens and write or draw your observations on the following page.

III. What Did You Discover?

❶ What are some of the differences that you observed between rocks and dirt?

_____

_____

❷ When you added water to the rock/dirt mixture, did the water get cloudy? If so, why do think that happened?

_____

_____

❸ When you allowed the rock/dirt mixture to settle, did you observe layers forming? If so, why do you think that happened?

_____

_____

❹ When you added the flour, did the flour form a layer as the mixture settled? Why or why not?

_____

_____

IV. Why?

In this experiment you observed the differences between rocks and dirt and how both rocks and dirt behave in a water mixture. When you mixed the rocks and dirt with water, you got what is called a slurry. When this slurry was allowed to settle, you noticed that the rocks settled first, and the lighter dirt particles settled last. When the flour was added, you could probably see a layer of flour settling between layers of rocks and dirt.

In your textbook you learned about sedimentary rocks. In this experiment you observed how sedimentary rocks are formed when sediments (rocks, dirt, and other particles) settle. The heavier particles will settle first, and the lighter particles will settle last. This causes layers to be formed.

Sedimentary rocks are formed when these layers are put under great pressure. When you see a sedimentary rock, you can observe different layers in the rock. These rock layers are created in the same way you created layers with your rock, dirt, flour, and water mixture.

V. Just For Fun

You can make your own edible sedimentary rock. Try the recipe below. Observe how the layers settle.

Get a cake mix and follow the directions on the package to make a batter. Before pouring the batter into a baking pan, stir in some nuts, gumdrops, and chocolate chips or M&Ms.

When you cut the cooled cake, observe the layers that have formed. In the box below, draw the cake and its layers.

EDIBLE SEDIMENTARY ROCK

Experiment 4

The Shape of Earth

I. Think About It

Why do you think the Earth is shaped like a slightly smashed ball that is a little farther across than it is from top to bottom? Write or draw your ideas below.

_____

_____

_____

_____

_____

II. Observe It

❶ Take a baseball and place it on the floor. Try to spin the ball in place.

❷ Write or draw your observations below.

_____

_____

_____

_____

❸ Fill a balloon with water, tie it closed, and place it on the floor.

❹ Without breaking the balloon, spin it in place. Write or draw your observations below.

_____

_____

_____

_____

_____

III. What Did You Discover?

❶ Did the baseball change shape when you spun it on the floor? Why or why not?

_____

_____

_____

❷ Did the water balloon change shape when you spun it on the floor? Why or why not?

_____

_____

_____

❸ Can you change the shape of the baseball with your hands? Why or why not?

_____

_____

_____

❹ Can you change the shape of the water balloon with your hands? Why or why not?

_____

_____

_____

IV. Why?

Since a baseball is solid all the way to its center, its shape cannot easily be changed. A water balloon has a soft center, which means that its shape can be more easily changed than can the shape of a baseball.

We live on the hard, rocky part of Earth (the crust), but Earth is mostly soft or fluid inside. The Earth spins around an axis, which is an imaginary straight line that goes through the center of the Earth. This spinning motion creates an outward-directed force called *centrifugal force*. Centrifugal force causes the Earth's center to bulge slightly as the soft part of the inner Earth is forced outward by centrifugal force.

In this experiment the balloon that holds the water is similar to the crust and outer mantle of the Earth. Both the balloon and the hard outer layers of Earth surround a soft center. As the balloon is spun, it is able to change in shape in response to centrifugal force. The crust and outer mantle and the soft part of the inner Earth have also changed in shape due to the centrifugal force caused by the spinning of the Earth. This has created the bulge at the equator of the Earth.

(See *Focus On Elementary Astronomy* for more about the effects of Earth's spin on its axis.)

V. Just For Fun

Sometimes a scientist will get an idea about what something is like or how it works and then will do an experiment by thinking about that idea and all its possibilities. This is called a *thought experiment*.

Here is a thought experiment for you to try. Use your imagination while doing this thought experiment. Write or draw your ideas on the next page.

THOUGHT EXPERIMENT

We have discovered that the Earth has a slightly flattened ball shape. Think about what it might be like if, instead of being round, the Earth were shaped like a cube.

Do you think anything would be different if Earth were shaped like a cube? Would travel be different? What would happen when you came to an edge or a corner? What things can you think of that might be different?

THOUGHT EXPERIMENT:
EARTH AS A CUBE

Experiment 5

Mud Volcanoes

In this experiment you will explore how the thickness of lava determines the type of mountain that can be formed by a volcano.

I. Think About It

❶ What happens when you pour thick syrup on your pancakes?

_____

_____

❷ How fast does it flow from the pancakes to the plate?

_____

_____

❸ What do you think would happen if you poured water on your pancakes?

_____

_____

❹ How fast do you think the water would flow from the pancakes to the plate?

_____

_____

❺ What happens when you mix dirt with a little bit of water? Does it make a good mud pie? Why or why not?

_____

_____

_____

❻ What happens when you mix dirt with a lot of water? Does it make a good mud pie? Why or why not?

_____

_____

_____

II. Observe It

I. Mix the following:

❶ .5 liter (about 2 cups) of dirt with .25 liter (about 1 cup) of water and label it "**A**.

❷ .5 liter (about 2 cups) of dirt with .5 liter (about 2 cups) of water and label it "**B**"

❸ .5 liter (about 2 cups) of dirt with .75 liter (about 3 cups) of water and label it "**C**"

II. Observe your three mixtures. In the chart below, write the answers to the following questions.

① Is the mixture thick or thin?

② Can you form a mud pie with the mixture? Why or why not?

③ Which is the thickest mixture?

④ Which is the thinnest mixture?

Question	A	B	C
①			
②			
③			
④			

III. Now take each mixture (**A**, **B**, and **C**) and pour a little of each on the ground. Pour each mixture in its own area and label each area **A**, **B**, or **C**.

Observe what happens. In the chart below, write the answers to the following questions.

① Is the mixture easy or difficult to pour?

② Does the mixture stay together or spread out? Why?

③ How far does each mixture spread?

Question	A	B	C
①			
②			
③			

IV. After you pour the mixtures, allow the three areas to dry out. Then add another layer to each area. Pour the same mixture over the same spot where you poured it the first time. Add more layers, letting each layer dry out before adding another.

Observe what happens. In the chart below, write the answers to the following questions.

① Does the mixture form layers?

② How high are 2, 3, or 4 layers of each mixture?

③ How wide are 2, 3, or 4 layers of each mixture?

④ How far does each mixture spread?

Question	A	B	C
①			
②			
③			
④			

III. What Did You Discover?

❶ Which was the thickest mixture?

_____

❷ Which was the thinnest mixture?

_____

❸ How easy was it to pour the thickest mixture? Why?

_____

_____

❹ How easy was it to pour the thinnest mixture? Why?

_____

_____

❺ Which of the 3 mixtures would make the best cone volcano? Why?

_____

_____

❻ Which of the 3 mixtures would make the best shield volcano? Why?

_____

_____

IV. Why?

Volcanic lava begins as magma in the mantle of the Earth. When the magma finds its way to the surface, it is called lava. Lava is an extremely hot mixture of melted rocks and minerals.

Some lava is thick like mixture **A**, and some lava is thin like mixture **C**. When thick lava comes out of a volcano, it can form a cone volcano with steep sides. Because the lava is thick, it won't flow very far from the center. When thin lava comes out of a volcano, it can form a shield volcano. Because the lava is thin, it can flow very far away from the center of the volcano.

V. Just For Fun

❶ Using thick mud, build a cone-shaped volcano.

❷ Before the mud dries, use a pencil to poke a hole down the center of the cone.

❸ Allow the mud to dry.

❹ When it is dry, pour 15 milliliters (1 tablespoon) of baking powder down the hole.

❺ Next, gently pour in 15 milliliters (1 tablespoon) of vinegar.

❻ Observe what happens and draw a picture of it.

MUD VOLCANO

Experiment 6

What's the Weather?

I. Think About It

❶ Do you think the sky looks different on different days? Why or why not?

_____

_____

❷ Do you think clouds always look the same? Why or why not?

_____

_____

❸ What do you think happens to plants when the wind blows hard?

_____

_____

❹ Do you think rain is important for plants? Why or why not?

_____

_____

❺ Do you think the weather changes the way animals behave? Why or why not?

_____

_____

_____

II. Observe It

Observe the weather every day for a week. Is it sunny? Cloudy? What do the clouds look like? Is it hot or cold? Is it raining or windy? What happens to the ground, the plants, and the animals as the weather changes?

In the following boxes, write or draw your observations.

DAY 1

Temperature _____

Observations

DAY 2

Temperature _____

Observations

DAY 3

Temperature _____

Observations

DAY 4

Temperature _____

Observations

DAY 5

Temperature _____

Observations

DAY 6

Temperature _____

Observations

DAY 7

Temperature _____

Observations

III. What Did You Discover?

❶ What changes in the weather were you able to observe?

_____

_____

❷ Did changes in the weather cause any changes in animal behavior? If so, what were they?

_____

_____

❸ Did changes in the weather affect the plants? If so, in what ways?

_____

_____

❹ Was the ground affected by the weather? How?

_____

_____

❺ In what ways did the weather affect your behavior and activities?

_____

_____

IV. Why?

Weather patterns change from hour to hour, day to day, and season to season.

The temperature of the atmosphere changes frequently. Energy from the Sun heats the atmosphere during the day. At night some of the heat is released back into space, making the air cooler.

The amount of moisture in the air also causes weather changes. When the air is dry, the sky is clear. When the air contains more water vapor, there are clouds. If there is a lot of water vapor, it may rain or snow, bringing water to plants and animals so they can live.

Winds can blow dirt around and even break or uproot plants. Extremely strong winds, like those in tornadoes and hurricanes, can move whole buildings!

Changes in the seasons also affect the weather. Summer and winter are caused by the tilt of the Earth toward or away from the Sun. (You can find out more about the tilt of the Earth in the *Focus On Elementary Astronomy Student Textbook.*)

All of these changes can affect how animals behave. They may be out looking for food, or they may be staying in trees or in their burrows, waiting for the weather to change.

V. Just For Fun

Make a wind tester!

Take a helium-filled balloon outside and find a place to tie it. Observe the balloon during the day. Does the balloon tell you anything about the wind? Why or why not? Draw or write your observations below.

How Fast Is Water?

I. Think About It

❶ When rain falls on the land, where do you think the rainwater goes?

_____

_____

❷ Does the kind of ground that rain falls on affect what happens to the rainwater? Why or why not?

_____

_____

❸ Do you think there is water under the ground? Why or why not?

_____

_____

❹ What do you think would happen to plants and animals if it did not rain? Why?

_____

_____

❺ Why do think rain makes mud puddles in some places but not others?

_____

_____

II. Observe It

❶ Take three Styrofoam cups and use a pencil to poke a hole in the bottom of each one.

❷ Measure about 237 milliliters (1 cup) of sand and pour it into one of the cups.

❸ Measure about 237 milliliters (1 cup) of pebbles and pour them into the second cup.

❹ Measure about 237 milliliters (1 cup) of small rocks and pour them into the third cup.

❺ Next, measure about 118 milliliters (4 ounces) of water and pour it into the cup containing the sand. Observe how long it takes the water to run through the sand.

❻ Write or draw your observations in the box provided on the next page. Write or draw anything else you observe.

❼ Repeat Steps ❺ & ❻ with the pebbles and then with the small rocks. Compare how long it takes the water to run through each cup.

How Quickly or Slowly Water Runs Through	
SAND	
PEBBLES	
SMALL ROCKS	

MORE OBSERVATIONS	
SAND	
PEBBLES	
SMALL ROCKS	

III. What Did You Discover?

❶ Which material did the water run through the fastest? Why?

_____

_____

_____

❷ Which material did the water run through the slowest? Why?

_____

_____

_____

❸ Do you think all of the water came out of the cup with the sand? Why or why not?

_____

_____

_____

❹ Do you think all of the water came out of the cup with the small rocks? Why or why not?

_____

_____

_____

IV. Why?

In this experiment the water ran through the pebbles and the small rocks faster than it did through the sand. This happens because the particles of sand are much smaller than the pebbles and rocks. The small size of the sand particles allows them to fit together closely, leaving less empty space for the water to flow through. The pebbles and rocks have bigger spaces between the pieces, so water can flow through more quickly. The amount of empty space between the particles of a material is called its *porosity*.

The type of ground that rain falls on affects how much water can go into the ground. If rain falls on ground made of pebbles or small rocks, the rainwater will quickly flow through it. Rainwater also flows fairly quickly through sand and may not leave much water on the surface for animals to drink.

Another kind of soil is called clay. Clay has very small particles with little space between them. It can take water a long time to go through clay. Rainwater tends to form puddles on this type of soil. Clay can make very slippery and sticky mud!

The best type of soil for plants is in between sandy soil and clay soil. This kind of soil allows rainwater to flow through it slowly, keeping enough water for plants to use for making food.

V. Just For Fun

Mud City!

Make a mud city using dirt, water, pebbles, and rocks. Using what you learned in the previous sections of this experiment, make rivers and a lake that holds water.

You can use pebbles, rocks, sand, or dirt for city walls or to contain the rivers and lake. Think about how you can make the water stay in the lake and what will make water flow in rivers. Can you add things that will make the water flow faster or slower or change direction?

Once you've built your city, you can make paper boats to float on the rivers and the lake.

What Do You See?

I. Think About It

❶ What living things do you think you will see if you walk around your yard and your neighborhood?

_____

_____

_____

_____

❷ What do you think these living things eat?

_____

_____

_____

❸ Where do you think these living things sleep?

_____

_____

_____

❹ Do you think you will see different plants and animals in different areas? Why or why not?

_____

_____

_____

II. Observe It

❶ Go for a walk around your yard and your neighborhood. Take this *Laboratory Workbook* with you so you can draw or write your observations.

❷ Carefully observe the environment you're in by walking slowly and looking up to the sky, down to the ground, and everywhere in between. Look at things close up and from farther away.

❸ Look for different animals, bugs, birds, plants, and people. Observe what they are doing. Are birds flying in the sky, singing in trees, or hopping in the grass? Is a dog taking its person for a walk? Are there flowers blooming? Is a squirrel chattering at you from a tree? Are there bugs crawling on plants? Do you see any animals, birds, or bugs eating? What are they eating?

Use the boxes on the next pages to draw or write what you see.

Observations of the Environment

Observations of the Environment

Observations of the Environment

III. What Did You Discover?

❶ Did you observe anything about the plants in your environment that you hadn't noticed before? What did you observe?

_____

_____

❷ What did you see animals doing?

_____

_____

❸ Were any of the living things eating? What and how were they eating?

_____

_____

❹ When you walked from one area of your environment to another, what differences in plants, animals, and birds did you observe?

_____

_____

❺ What did you see that was surprising?

_____

_____

IV. Why?

The biosphere contains all the living things on Earth. Within the biosphere are different areas called environments. Each environment has a particular set of resources that make it possible for certain living things to live in that area. For example, a desert environment is a good home for lizards, cacti, and other animals and plants that don't need much water. An ocean environment is where you will find plants, fish, and animals, such as whales and dolphins, that can live in salty water. There are pine forest environments, mountain environments, lake and river environments, coastal environments, plains environments, and many others.

The region where you live has its own environment. The weather, amount of rainfall, type of soil, variations in temperature, plants, animals, and insects all work together to create this environment.

An environment can be any size. As you were making observations on your walk, you may have noticed that certain plants grow best in one area but not another, and certain animals live in one area but not another. This is a result of differences within the larger environment. Each plant and animal grows best when it finds just the right conditions to live in.

V. Just For Fun

An exoplanet is a planet that is orbiting a different sun (star) than ours. (See *Focus On Elementary Astronomy* for more about exoplanets.)

Imagine you are the first astronaut to land on the exoplanet Kepler-62e in the constellation Lyra. Suppose you discover that Kepler-62e has a biosphere.

What do you think you would see when you land? Do you think Kepler-62e would look like Earth or be very different? Would there be an atmosphere with clouds? What would they look like? Would you find water? Where would the water be found? Would there be lots of plants and animals? What would the plants look like? What would the animals look like? What would they be doing? What would they eat? Would there be human-like creatures? What would they look like? What would they be doing? What else do you think you would see on Kepler-62e?

On the next page draw or write what you imagine the biosphere on Kepler-62e would look like.

A Visit to Kepler-62e

Experiment 9

Moving Iron

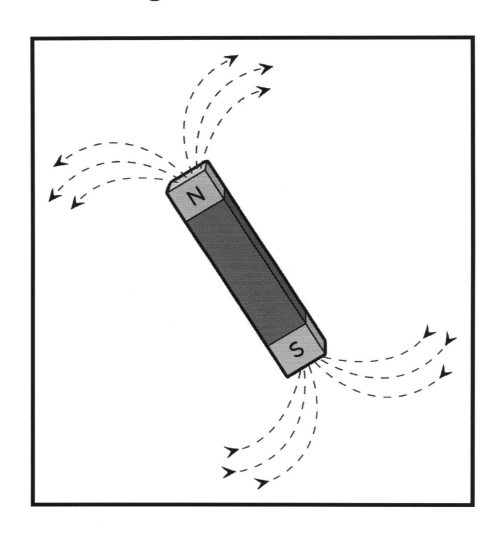

I. Think About It

❶ Do you think if you look at a magnet you will see its magnetic forces? Why or why not?

_____

_____

_____

❷ Do you think magnetic forces can be useful? Why or why not?

_____

_____

_____

❸ If you have two magnets, do you think you could make the two north poles stick together? Why or why not?

_____

_____

_____

❹ Do you think there is a way to show that Earth has a magnetic field surrounding it? Why or why not?

_____

_____

_____

II. Observe It

❶ Pour Karo syrup into the box until there is about 6 millimeters (1/4") of syrup covering the bottom.

❷ Put the bar magnet on the table and place the box on top of it so the magnet is about in the center of the box.

❸ Carefully pour the iron filings on top of the syrup.

❹ Wait 30 minutes and then check the iron filings.

❺ In the box below, draw what the iron filings look like.

III. What Did You Discover?

❶ What did the iron filings look like when you first put them in the syrup?

_____

_____

❷ What did the iron filings look like after 30 minutes?

_____

_____

❸ What do you think made the iron filings move?

_____

_____

❹ Do you think if you did this experiment again, the iron filings would end up in the same pattern? Why or why not?

_____

_____

❺ What do you think this experiment might tell you about Earth's magnetic field?

_____

_____

_____

IV. Why?

A magnetic field is the area around a magnet that is affected by magnetic forces. In this experiment you were able to "see" the magnetic field around your magnet by observing how it affected the iron filings.

Earth has a magnetic field similar to the one that affected the iron filings in the experiment. Earth's magnetic field points out from the north pole, surrounds the Earth, and points in at the south pole. Earth's magnetic field is different from that of a bar magnet because it is created by swirling molten metals in Earth's core rather than from a solid bar of metal.

Another difference is that Earth's magnetic field extends into space and is affected by energy from the Sun. When the Sun's energy hits the magnetic field, it creates the magnetosphere. The magnetosphere, in turn, lets enough heat and light energy through to keep plants and animals healthy. At the same time, it stops too much energy from getting to Earth. Life could not exist if too much of the Sun's energy reached the surface of Earth, so the magnetosphere is essential for life to continue to exist.

V. Just For Fun

❶ Try moving the box so the magnet is in a different position under it. Wait about 30 minutes, then look at the pattern the iron filings make. Did repositioning the magnet make a difference?

In the box below draw the pattern made by the iron filings.

MAGNETIC FIELD
Magnet Repositioned

❷ Place a second magnet under the box. Wait about 30 minutes. Does having two magnets change the magnetic field?

Draw your observations below.

MAGNETIC FIELD
2 Magnets

❸ Try moving the two magnets to different positions. Wait about 30 minutes each time, then check to see what the pattern of the iron filings looks like.

Draw your observations below.

MAGNETIC FIELD
2 Magnets Repositioned

What Do You Need?

I. Think About It

❶ Do you think a plant needs the atmosphere in order to live and grow? Why or why not?

_____

_____

_____

❷ Do you think a plant needs the hydrosphere in order to live and grow? Why or why not?

_____

_____

_____

❸ Do you think a plant needs the biosphere in order to live and grow? Why or why not?

_____

_____

_____

❹ Do you think a plant needs the geosphere in order to live and grow? Why or why not?

_____

_____

_____

II. Observe It

Plant a garden!

❶ Decide what kind of plant you want to grow and then get seeds for it.

❷ Plant several seeds outdoors in a garden. If you don't have space for a garden, you can use a flower pot, milk carton, or other container.

❸ Water the seeds when you plant them and then check the soil daily. When it starts to get dry, add more water.

❹ Write or draw your observations in the following boxes. Each box can have observations for more than one day.

❺ As your plant gets bigger, what do you observe about its growth? How fast is it growing? Is it staying healthy? Is it getting too much or too little water or sunshine? Are bugs eating the plant? If so, what do they look like? Do you see any worms in the soil? Are any animals or birds affecting your plant? What else can you observe?

❻ Write or draw your observations as the plant grows. As you make observations about your plant, think about which of Earth's parts is affecting it and in what way. Is it the biosphere, hydrosphere, atmosphere, geosphere, or magnetosphere, or is it a combination of two or more of these?

GROWING A PLANT

GROWING A PLANT

GROWING A PLANT

GROWING A PLANT

III. What Did You Discover?

❶ How easy or difficult was it to grow your plant? Why?

_____

_____

_____

❷ Did your plant get enough water from rain? How could you tell?

_____

_____

_____

❸ Did your plant have any problems with bugs? Why or why not?

_____

_____

_____

❹ Were any animals helpful or harmful to your plant? Why or why not?

_____

_____

_____

❺ Was there enough sunlight for your plant? How can you tell?

_____

_____

_____

❻ Was the soil you used good for your plant to grow in? Why or why not?

_____

_____

_____

❼ In what ways do you think the different parts of the Earth worked together to help your plant grow?

_____

_____

_____

_____

_____

_____

IV. Why?

For a plant to grow, all the different parts of the Earth have to work together. The plant is part of the biosphere and so are the bugs, animals, and people that might eat the plant. Bacteria in the soil fix nitrogen for plants to use, and worms add nutrients to the soil.

Earth's geosphere provides soil that has minerals the plant needs for making food. The soil also contains water that is taken up by the plant's roots. The soil provides a place for roots to anchor the plant to the ground so it won't blow away in the wind.

The hydrosphere provides the water needed by the plant, whether it comes from rain or from your garden hose. The hydrosphere works with the atmosphere to make clouds that move over the Earth, carrying rain to different parts of the land.

The atmosphere has carbon dioxide for the plant to use to make food. The gases in the atmosphere hold onto some of the heat energy from the Sun, helping to keep Earth warm at night. Also, the atmosphere lets light energy from the Sun reach Earth so plants can use the Sun's energy for making food.

The magnetosphere protects the plant from getting too much energy from the Sun, which would be harmful.

If any one of these parts of Earth were missing, plants could not live and grow.

V. Just For Fun

Grow an herb garden!

Herbs are plants that are great for adding extra flavor to salads, soups, and other foods. Sometimes they are used to make delicious teas and for medicines.

Herbs can be grown outdoors in pots or in a garden bed, and many can be grown in small pots indoors.

Decide which herbs you would like to grow. You might look for information about herbs in the library or online. Or you might want to choose them by names that sound interesting or by what the plants in the store look like. Some possibilities are: basil, rosemary, thyme, chervil, lemon balm, oregano, parsley, dill, spearmint, chamomile. If you have a cat, it might enjoy having some catnip.

Once you have decided which herbs you want to grow, get seeds or small plants.

Tend your herb garden, and when the plants are big enough, gather some leaves to put in your salad and soup. While you and your family are eating the tasty herbs, you can tell everyone how all the parts of the Earth worked together to bring each plant's unique flavor to you—Earth's geosphere, biosphere, hydrosphere, atmosphere, and magnetosphere all helped out!

36448378R00062

Made in the USA
Charleston, SC
05 December 2014